Tales of Heaven and Earth

Sophie Pommier is an Arabic scholar,
a specialist on the Islamic world,
and the author of several books
about Muslim societies.

Cover design by Peter Bennett

Extracts from the Qur'an are from
the translation from the Arabic by NJ Dawood,
first published by Penguin Books Ltd in 1956.

ISBN: 1 85103 242 8
© Editions Gallimard, 1995
Managing editor: Jacqueline Vallon
English text © 1995 by Moonlight Publishing Ltd
First published in the United Kingdom 1996
by Moonlight Publishing Ltd, 36 Stratford Road, London W8
Printed in Italy by Editoriale Zanardi

Muhammad's Night Journey

by Sophie Pommier

Illustrated by Marie Mallard

Translated by Gwen Marsh

Moonlight Publishing

For Henri and Léo

One night the Angel Gabriel wakes Muhammad...

Islam, meaning submission to God, is the name of the religion believed to have been completed by Muhammad.

When merchants set off to cross the desert they travelled together in groups that formed caravans. The caravaneers led dromedaries that carried the merchandise.

Makkah was already a busy pilgrimage centre in Muhammad's time. There, in the sanctuary of the Ka'bah, the Black Stone was kept. It was said to have been given to Adam, who set it in the Ka'bah, a cube-shaped building now covered in a black cloth on which verses from the Qur'an are embroidered in gold.

This story tells of Muhammad, the Prophet of Islam, when he was a caravaneer in Makkah, a holy place famous for the sanctuary of the Black Stone, called the Ka'bah.

It was the middle of the night but Muhammad was too excited to sleep. Some time before, the Angel Gabriel had appeared to him and had revealed to him the words of God. His heart was full of this revelation and he was eager to pass it on as the Angel had told him to. But now he was worried because, when he had called together his

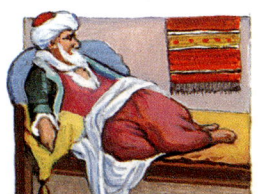

...and invites him to ride a horse from heaven, the mare al-Buraq.

Quraysh, which means little shark in Arabic, was the name of a tribe of powerful merchants in Makkah.

Quraysh people and told them God's words, he had been met with blank stares. Most of them simply did not believe him. These traders understood about the value of goods and the care of camels, but they could not grasp the importance of Muhammad's message and his talk of one God.

At last Muhammad fell into a heavy sleep.

There was a rustling sound, as of wings sweeping the air, and a sense of a presence disturbing his rest. The Angel Gabriel was again by his side. His face was white as snow, his hair like coral. His clothes were streaming with whiteness as if formed from moonlight, sparkling with pearls and precious stones and held by two golden bands. The Angel's hands were like flames and his wings and feet seemed like tender green shoots of grass. He was a shaft of pure light in the depths of the night.

"Arise, Messenger of God," the heavenly figure commanded. The Prophet stood to answer the call.

Then from the shadows of the night a marvellous creature materialised: a winged beast, smaller than a mule, but larger than a donkey. Fine pearls beaded her mane, emeralds her hair and rubies her tail.

"Mount this animal, friend of God. Her name is al-Buraq and she can fly faster than lightning."

Angels are creatures who serve God. Some take messages to men. Gabriel was the angel sent by God to Muhammad to reveal to him God's words to be written as the Qur'an.

Al-Buraq, meaning flash or spark in Arabic, is the name of this odd animal with the body of a mare, the head of a human being, and the tail of a peacock.

Islam regards Moses, to whom the Torah of the Jews was revealed, as a divine messenger.

Moses brought the Children of Israel out of Egypt and received the Ten Commandments on Mount Sinai.

Muhammad obeyed the Angel. As he stepped up to this fantastic creature, al-Buraq knelt for her rider to mount and spread her wings with their many feathers. Each step covered a greater distance than even the keen eye of a hawk can scan. But the Angel Gabriel, escorting him on his right, suddenly stopped this night flight: it was fitting that Muhammad should pause to worship God at Mount Sinai where Moses had received the Creator's commandments. Further on, where the earth received Jesus' body, Muhammad paused again to pray to God. Then once more the wide starlit spaces of the night were speeding past. The Prophet heard a faint murmur in his ear: "Stop, man of God. I will enrich your soul with advice." The voice came out of the limitless void but Muhammad chose to ignore it. So also he was deaf to another voice from another part of the sky: "Halt, Oh Muhammad, be wise and pay heed to my words."

In Arabic God is named Allah. Islam has 99 other 'beautiful names' for God: each evokes an attribute of God – the Merciful, the Just, the Maker of the Worlds, and so on.

For Islam, Jesus is a prophet, born of a virgin consecrated to God, but he is not God's son. Allah substituted another man on the cross and took Jesus into heaven. At the end of time he will return.

Skimming through the clouds at great speed, al-Buraq and her rider had already come far. The voices had died away in the night like dead stars. Then a woman of inexpressible beauty appeared. With her hair spread loose on her shoulders and gems of all colours on her robes, she put out her arms towards the Prophet. But Muhammad ignored her, and al-Buraq seemed moved by some higher will and bore her rider on. At last the flight came to an end. As Muhammad dismounted a young man, handsome and perfumed, embraced him warmly – then vanished.

The Prophet was intrigued by these strange encounters and plied Gabriel with questions. "The first voice you heard would have told you of Christianity," explained the Angel. "If you'd stopped, your people would have become Christians. The second voice was that of the Jewish law. Had you responded you would have led your people into Judaism. The woman with flowing hair simply sought to distract you from spiritual values by the worldly charms of Here Below. But the young man's welcome is the embrace of the true religion of Allah."

With these words Gabriel led Muhammad into the precincts of the Temple of Holy Jerusalem. Here he was

Christianity is the religion of those who believe that Jesus is the Son of God, and is the Messiah.

Worldly charms Here Below means of the earth, as distinct from the Beyond, meaning heaven, or the Most High, meaning God.

In a flash the Prophet finds himself in the Temple of Jerusalem.

offered a tray with three cups: the first with wine, the second, water and the third, milk. The Prophet chose the milk, drank some and replaced the cup.

"Praised be your choice," Gabriel said. "If you'd drunk the fruit of the vine your people would have been lost in the mists of drunkenness. If you'd taken the cup of water they would have been drowned in the depths of sin. But milk guarantees the salvation of your brothers. Had you emptied the cup all would have been saved."

"Give me back the cup," begged Muhammad, "that I may finish what I started."

"That is not in my power," Gabriel replied gently. "The ink of the Book of Destiny is indelible and what is written is written."

In the Temple precincts, the Prophet found himself in the midst of a strange and illustrious company.

Among God's angels were the Prophets of old. Allah that day had opened their tombs so that they could join in honouring the man whose word would finally prove the strength of the message to which each of them had contributed a part. They all greeted him and he returned their greeting. Gabriel came forward and in a resounding voice called all to prayer. Then he turned to Muhammad:

Muslims call Jerusalem Al Quods, meaning 'the Holy Place' in Arabic.

Wine is forbidden in Islam. "The sin found therein is greater than its usefulness," says the Qu'ran (II, 219). Wine is associated with Paradise, but the mystical intoxication of the love of God is just a literary expression.

Milk is the primordial food, symbol of life, fertility and knowledge.

The Book of Destiny records the life of every human being as preordained by God.

All the Prophets are assembled there to pay homage to him.

A Mu'adhdhin calls prayer five times a day. This is one of the Five Pillars of Islam. The others are: profession of faith, fasting for Ramadan, pilgrimage to Makkah, giving welfare to the poor (zakah).

Prayer is led by an Imam, a leader.

Abraham is considered a most devout Muslim: he obeyed God to the point of sacrificing his son, Isaac.

"Lead the prayer, Oh Master of all the Prophets, Leader of all peoples." This Muhammad did.

The prophets lined up in rows behind him, the Imam. They expressed their joy at his glory and prayed that the Most High confer grace upon him. Their prayers went up to heaven in a long chain, generation after generation:

"Blessed be God Who made me with His hands, caused the angels to bow before me and from my loins brought forth the line of the Prophets." So spoke Adam.

"Blessed be God Who saved me from the waters and gave me the gift of prophecy." So spoke Noah.

"Blessed be God Who made me His friend, conferred great power on me, used me as His Messenger and spared me the bite of fire." So spoke Abraham.

"Blessed be God Who chose me among men to broadcast His words and Who revealed the Torah to me." So spoke Moses.

"Blessed be God Who inspired my Psalms and made iron obedient in my hand." So spoke David.

"Blessed be God Who gave me power over the winds, genies and men, and taught me the language of birds." So spoke Solomon.

"Blessed be God Who has made me His Word, made me guardian of the Scriptures and of wisdom, by my hand

Noah is popular in Islam; he is quoted in the Qur'an, where the story of the Flood is told, as in the Bible.

The Qur'an teaches that Adam was the first man, sent as God's envoy to earth. God revealed to him the names of things so that he could teach the angels.

The Law that God gave to Moses is in the Torah. It is a holy book, and is the basis of Judaism.

All gather around Muhammad singing glory to Allah.

Conqueror of Goliath, David defeated the Philistines and succeeded Saul, King of Israel. He is said to be the author of the Book of Psalms.

The Qur'an describes Jesus as the 'Word of God' bestowed on Mary (4: 171), and sent to take God's words to the Children of Israel (61: 6).

healed the lepers and the blind man, by my voice brought back to life those who had died, and protected me from the grip of Satan." So spoke Jesus.

"Blessed be God Who has made me His Messenger to carry His message and warning to all mankind. He has dictated the Qur'an to me which holds the key to every question and has placed my people above others. He has made me the Seal of the Prophets." Thus spoke Muhammad.

Solomon is regarded in Islam as a prophet and a wise king, with great powers, including speaking to birds and other creatures. The Qur'an also tells of his meeting with Bilqis, Queen of Sheba.

For Muslims, Muhammad is the Seal of the Prophets, the one who completes the Revelation of the one God which was begun by earlier prophets.

Gabriel invites Muhammad to climb up a ladder.

Green is a colour favoured in Islam. It is the colour of water and of oases, and so symbolises great material and spiritual riches, and thus salvation.

The ladder is a symbol of the way up towards God. It is an image also found in the Bible and throughout the Christian tradition.

Leaving the Temple, Gabriel led Muhammad to the foot of a ladder. The ladder was covered in rich green velvet, which itself dazzled the eye, but the rungs glistened with thousands of gems: rubies, topazes, emeralds, pearls, silver and gold. With Gabriel and the angels guarding the ladder, the Prophet went up a few steps.

But here a strange sight met his eye. An angel of terrifying aspect loomed over him from a throne of light, on his right a wooden table, on his left a huge tree. Two groups of angels formed his retinue. The first, on his right, shone with a soft radiance and exhaled a subtle

perfume. The faces of the others, on his left, were blacker than ink. Their eyes glowed red like burning coals. From them came a foul odour and their voices were as thunder. "The seated angel is called 'Azra'il," said Gabriel, "and he is the Prince of Death. The mortality of all human life is shown to him by the tree growing beside him: each of its leaves bears the name of a man or woman. When the life of that being comes to its end, the leaf withers and dies. At the same moment, in the great register of names that stands on the wooden table, the entry concerning the deceased darkens. The book also tells the fate awaiting them. The angels of light take charge of those who are among the chosen and a jade-coloured bird carries their souls to Paradise. The black angels treat the wicked ruthlessly, their death is pronounced forthwith and their breath violently snatched from them."

Now, with Gabriel, Muhammad went on into seven heavens, strange places above the sky before Paradise itself. The first, the iron heaven, was peopled with curious creatures, part human, part beast and eagle. Here Muhammad met John and Jesus. The second heaven was of copper. The angels there were seventy thousand times greater than those in the first heaven. They carried swords and lances and green

Jade is a green stone. It is often a symbol of perfection because it is so beautiful.

John the Baptist, Jesus' cousin, baptised people in the river Jordan.

Gabriel shows Muhammad the seven heavens.

The Night of Destiny, which marks the beginning of the Revelation made to Muhammad through the Angel Gabriel, is celebrated on the 27th night of the month of Ramadan.

Jacob, son of Isaac, was Abraham's grandson.

Enoch was the son of Cain and father of Methuselah (Genesis, ch.5. v.24). Elias was a prophet of the 9th century BC, often shown riding up to heaven in a chariot of fire.

banners. These were angels of the Night of Destiny, who bring peace to believers.

In the golden heaven a mighty angel held on his right thumb all the freshwater rivers of the world, and on his left thumb the salt waters.

In the emerald heaven was a fleet of armed angels with horses' heads, ready to fly to the rescue of any believer in difficulty. For this, each one could call upon seventy thousand steeds that were always kept harnessed.

When describing his journey afterwards Muhammad said that when he had seen the Prophets in Jerusalem it was as they appeared on earth but now he saw them transfigured into celestial beings. Thus, in the various heavens he saw David and Solomon and also handsome Joseph, son of Jacob, whose face, he said, was radiant like the full moon. He saw the venerable Enoch and Elias in the silver heaven. Moses he recognised by his long hair and majestic bearing, and he said of Moses' brother Aaron, how beautiful he was, seated on a throne of light, his beard half white, half black and a diadem on his brow. Seventy thousand winged creatures with eagles' heads surrounded him.

The seventh heaven was of rubies. It is impossible to describe what the Prophet saw there because God

An angel carries a just man's soul to Paradise (18th-century manuscript).

Facing page: the Prophet ascends to heaven (18th-century Arab miniature).

In Islam, God appointed Aaron as a prophet to help his brother Moses as spokesman.

Visions of heaven pass before the Prophet's dazzled eyes.

An angel with 70,000 heads (from the Miraj-nameh, a 15th-century manuscript).

commanded him not to tell. All we know is that he led the prayer and met Adam, father of mankind.

The summit of their ascent was a superb jujube tree known as the Tree of the Uttermost End. In its shade the two travellers rested. This tree marked the furthest point beyond which no-one, not even an angel, was permitted to go. From its strong roots flowed the river of Grace and the river of Mercy, into whose water Gabriel and Muhammad plunged one after the other. From drops showering off the archangel's wings seventy thousand cherubim were born.

Suddenly the voice of God called to Muhammad to approach. His heart beat wildly, for God was all-powerful, transcendant, above human nature, beyond the grasp of the human spirit. Gabriel calmed his fears and gave him courage but, as he had no permission to go on himself, the Chosen of God went on alone.

Muhammad found himself rising through great spaces and over strange plains along the shores of seas of light and seas of darkness. Echoing across the unfathomable void came the Voice of the All High. Three times it summoned him to come near. Muhammad closed his eyes, for the inexpressible vision was more than his eyes

The jujube tree is a thorny tree with edible fruit. In Islam it represents the limit, the measure or scope of time and space.

Muslims must wash before they pray. These rites wash off the dust of the road but also the 'dust' of sin so that a person can enter into prayer with a clean body and a pure heart.

Suddenly the voice of the All High summons him to approach.

could bear. His Lord placed His hand on him to calm him. From the foot of the divine throne the Prophet saluted God and received a reply of blessing.

"My God, what will you give my people as proof of Your love?" he asked.

His God answered: "Last and best of the Prophets, your people profess their faith with the words: 'There is no other god but God'.

They will now add: 'and Muhammad is his Messenger', then all faults will be wiped from the records."

"My God, what other favour will You grant us?"

"I pardon seventy thousand times seventy thousand of your people. I pardon the rebel who returns to the true faith. I pardon a hundred thousand of the damned who are born to your people. But hear

Seventy thousand, in the Bible, expresses universality. This number, like seven and some of its multiples, is often found in Islam to convey totality.

Admitted alone to the ineffable Presence, Muhammad talks with his God.

now, Oh Muhammad, the orders I impose on Muslims: fifty times a day you will send your prayers up to Me."

The Prophet was too grateful for the grace accorded his people to dare to protest. Yet fifty prayers seemed such a heavy burden for weak human shoulders to bear.

Busy with these thoughts he continued his journey. On his way he met Moses again who confirmed his fears: such a great burden of prayer would be too much for humankind. Bravely Muhammad returned to the All Powerful to speak for his people: "My God, you have ordered fifty prayers for believers. Could you not reduce this command?"

The reply came: "So be it. I reduce that obligation by ten prayers."

On Moses' advice Muhammad three times asked for a reduction in this ritual duty. Three times Allah met his demands until he was satisfied with five daily prayers. Then Muhammad resumed his journey down to lower regions.

A Muslim supplicating to Allah (from the Miraj-nameh, 15th-century manuscript).

Saying five daily prayers is one of the five duties that a good Muslim must observe. Islam commends self-control but not efforts beyond human capability.

Calligraphy is a major art in Islam. Above, a calligrapher with his tools: penknife, pens made of reeds, inkwell. Below, Allah is referred to by different names – Allah the Beautiful, the Gracious, the Merciful, the Forgiving...

... and Him, indicating God's uniqueness.

Having rejoined Gabriel, Muhammad sets off to Paradise.

Paradise (a word of Persian origin meaning garden) is referred to in the Qur'an simply as al-Jannah, or garden. The same term is used also for the Garden of Eden where Adam and Eve lived.

Muhammad, in the company of Gabriel, continued his journey towards Paradise. They came to a sparkling sea that seemed endless. Beyond stretched a sea of shadows and beyond that a sea of fire, then a range of mountains whose slopes ran down to the shore of the sea of seas.

This was the domain of a huge creature, a cockbird whose claws gripped the depths of Hell while its crest reached the throne of God, the Creator and Sustainer of the world. The span of its multicoloured wings was the measure of the entire universe. Its feathers were

The cock's crow at sunrise is regarded as a sign of Allah's glory and wisdom. It announces dawn. "The white rooster is my friend," says Muhammad. "It is the enemy of God's enemy." (Hadith)

encrusted with topazes, pearls and rubies set on a down of sparkling green. This bird repeats unceasingly the praises of its Creator and on earth the cockcrow that everywhere greets the dawn echoes His praise in unison.

The two companions came to the borders of Paradise. No human eye could measure the height of the wall around it. The cornerstones were alternately gold and silver. The bricks were of white pearl, topazes and emeralds, held by a cement made of a mixture of amber and musk ground up in rose water. Beyond this wall lay the garden of eternity.

This Paradise was watered by four rivers that sprang from an immense cupola of white pearls with a door of emerald and a lock of gold. The first river, flowing east, was a river of honey. The second, flowing west, was a river of milk. The waters of the third, flowing south, were totally transparent and tasted exquisite. The fourth and last river was of wine and flowed north. Once they left Paradise these rivers flowed on over the earth. Their names on earth are: the Nile, the Tigris, the Euphrates and the Djayhun and on earth they become

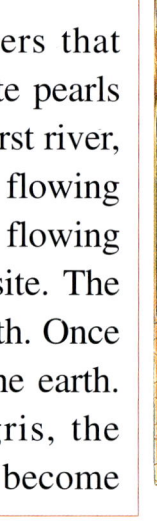

Topaz and ruby are gemstones, the first yellow, the second red. Red is said to evoke the happiness of ancient times.

In the garden of delights, he discovers the pleasures awaiting the Fortunate.

familiar rivers of water.

There were seven paradises with dazzling cities, castles, palaces and houses of pure light and splendour. Maidens were there, well admired, of a beauty past all imagining. Their perfume was so fine that, simply by inhaling it, a sick person would be cured. No earthly voice or instrument pleased the ear once the song of these beautiful women had been heard. Each of them had the name of her spouse written on her bosom; their hearts were so transparent that they could not think a single thought not shared by the spouse.

The garden of delights was the highest of the paradises, the one chosen by God for His prophet's dwelling. Muhammad learned here the fate awaiting the Fortunate, the true believers who also obeyed God.

On entering Paradise the righteous would bathe to rid their soul of sin and their body of dirt. They would be presented to their spouses and taken to their dwelling. Then they would gather together beneath the Tree of Felicity from which sprang fountains of wine, and there listen to the greeting from the angels.

Marvellous camels would be brought to them, made of jacinth, to conduct them into God's Presence. The All Merciful would reveal Himself to them and would

The Djayhun is a river in Central Asia.

Jacinth is a yellowish-red precious stone, originally from Sri Lanka, and much traded since ancient times.

Seven is a holy number, symbol of fullness, perfection and achievement.

Pleasures between husband and wife can be enjoyed in Paradise. The Qur'an prefers polygamy (more than one wife) to adultery (partners outside marriage) which it strongly condemns. The Qur'an imposes conditions for polygamy and restricts the number of wives a man can take.

Muhammad visits the place that will be his own for all eternity.

promise them everlasting delights.

For the Prophet of Islam favours would be even greater. Gabriel took Muhammad to see the sumptuous place that would be his, a palace of crystal built on pillars of gold and silver, beside a lake whose waters were so clear they were perfectly transparent. But the two travellers could not remain here long, as the Angel was charged with the mission to take his companion to see Hell as well as heaven.

Fortunate ones accompanied by their houris (women of celestial beauty promised to the pious), from the Miraj-nameh (15th century).

Muhammad explores the seven parts of Hell.

In deserts where plant life is sparce nothing stops the wind; it creates sandstorms, and sand fills every cranny, making the earth barren.

Muhammad was astonished to find that beneath the world of men were seven lower worlds, one below another, all made of fire and heat. Through Gabriel God taught his Messenger the secrets of Hell's geography: "The first region is called the Region of Ashes. On the Day of Judgment it will let loose a barren wind whose sharp breath will reduce to nothing all structures natural or human: mountains, towns, or castles. And this scorching wind will flay the flesh of the damned.

"The second region is called the Hard Region. The soil

In his poem *The Divine Comedy*, Dante (1265–1321) describes nine circles of Hell which he visits with the Latin poet Virgil (below, after Botticelli, late 14th century). Dante's account was much influenced by Muslim literature on Muhammad's night journey.

there is infested with scorpions whose stings are as long and sharp as lances. They sieze the sinners by the hair, strip off their skins and pump them full of their poison. The wretches finish as dislocated puppets; then the All Powerful restores them to their original state so that their suffering will begin again and know no end.

"The third region is called the Region of Misfortune. Hideous beasts skulk here, whose searing bite reduces the sinners to liquid and leaves them like melted wax.

"The fourth region, called the Barren Region, is inhabited by monstrous serpents. Better to endure a thousand deaths than one of their stings.

"The fifth region is called the Smooth Region; it is covered with stones of sulphur. The angels are charged with hanging one of these round the neck of each sinner before taking him to Hell. Once there, the stone bursts into flame and turns the sufferer into a human torch.

"The sixth region is called the Far Distant Place. It contains the registers in which are recorded the sins of mankind. Here are seas of pitch that can dissolve any rock in an instant, even a rock the size of a large mountain. When sinners are thrown into it their insides are destroyed.

"The seventh region, the Astounding Region, is the realm

The scorpion, whose sting is fatal, is a symbol of evil.

The stone of sulphur or pyrites, is also called fools' gold because it is yellow and glitters, and looks slightly like gold.

God told the angels to prostrate themselves before him. Iblis became a demon because he refused.

Muslims have two judgments. First, in the grave, an angel comes to find out if the person was a good believer. The departed soul is brought back to the body and the dead person has some comfort or punishment until the Day of the Last Judgment.

of the Devil himself."

Muhammad did not forget that he had a mission to report to mankind all that he had seen and learned about the mysteries of the Hereafter. The Last Judgment was terrifying to think of, but Muhammad asked Gabriel about it.

"On the Day of the Last Judgment," replied the winged messenger, "the Beast with thirty thousand times thirty thousand teeth, that lurks hidden at the heart of the infernal regions, will escape from its guards and fall upon men, spitting flames and suffocating fumes. The people will fall to their knees as the Beast gallops towards them full of destructive rage. But you, Oh Muhammad, will seize it by the bridle and order it back to its lair to wait until the wicked are duly delivered to it when their fate is decided. And it will obey you.

"Men and women will be summoned to appear and will gather naked and barefoot. At the end of an interminable time, the Eternal One will, in all His glory, command that great scales be brought to him, scales as wide as the space between East and West. Each human being will be called by name and must go to the scales carrying two buckets. Into the right-hand tray, shining like a diamond, will be poured the bucket containing the good actions

This Beast ready to fall upon men is like the symbolic monster desribed in the Apocalypse, the last book in the Christian Bible.

He has to endure the sight of the torments of the damned...

done during the person's earthly life. Into the left-hand tray, as dark as deepest night, the contents of the second bucket will be poured: all the sins he or she has committed, except those already forgiven. Weighing the two provides the verdict: chosen or condemned.

"After this first test everyone will then face the crossing of the As-Sirat bridge. Finer than a hair and sharper than a sword blade, this bridge spans the fires of Hell; it is surrounded by barriers of fire and straddles abysses full of a thousand terrifying instruments with pincers and snapping jaws. Believers who hope for Paradise will be able to show the exact measure of their faith and respond as true Muslims to all ordeals, and therefore will be able to reach the other side.

"Some will pass but many will fall. They will fall into Jahannam, a place of total darkness, made of the wrath of God. It has seven gates, one above another, like burning brands. The first is for those who worship idols. The second is for those who start following the Law of God but turn aside. The third is for those who amass wealth dishonestly; the fourth for gamblers, trouble-makers and blasphemers; the fifth for those who neglect prayers and refuse alms to the poor. The sixth is for those who

In the Christian tradition too, the scales illustrate the scene of the Last Judgment. Here the scales are held by Michael (from a Spanish painting of the 13th century).

The crossing of the As-Sirat bridge is a way of making sure whether the believer has taken the Right Way as taught by God in the Qur'an – the way of Islam.

Already in ancient Egypt the weighing of souls was a test awaiting the dead in the Hereafter. The *Book of the Dead* shows how to succeed.

...so he can tell the faithful and stop them straying from the Right Way.

Jahannam is one of the words for Hell. It was originally a Christian word and comes from the name of a place of sacrifice, Gue-Hennam, near Jerusalem.

question the message of the Qur'an and the seventh for those who are guilty of fraud. God will every day gather together demons and the damned at each gate and force them to contemplate the delights of Paradise forever denied them."

Muhammad witnessed the sufferings of the wretched human creatures delivered to the torments their misdeeds had earned for them: he saw immodest or quarrelsome women devoured by flames and thrashed by angels; he saw men who broke their word and those who made mischief writhing in agony, eternally damned...

"What you have seen and learned," said Gabriel, "you must pass on to your people. You must bear witness to the truth of it so that they may keep to the Right Way and justify the favours the All Merciful has granted them. Now you must go back to your people."

To remain in the *Right Way* of Islam a person must believe in Allah and his Prophet Muhammad, do good, that is, do Allah's will, and avoid evil, that is, avoid what Allah has forbidden.

Back in Makkah, the Prophet recounts his adventures.

Gabriel brought Muhammad back to the rock in front of the Temple in Jerusalem from which he had begun his ascension to heaven. Al-Buraq awaited him there and together they returned to Makkah, arriving there a little before dawn. Muhammad went back to the house of his cousin, Umm Hani', where he had led the faithful in prayer the previous night. He woke up the people and again led them in the dawn prayer. Turning to Umm Hani', he said, "I prayed here with you last night, then I went to Jerusalem and prayed there, and now I have

prayed with you the morning prayer."

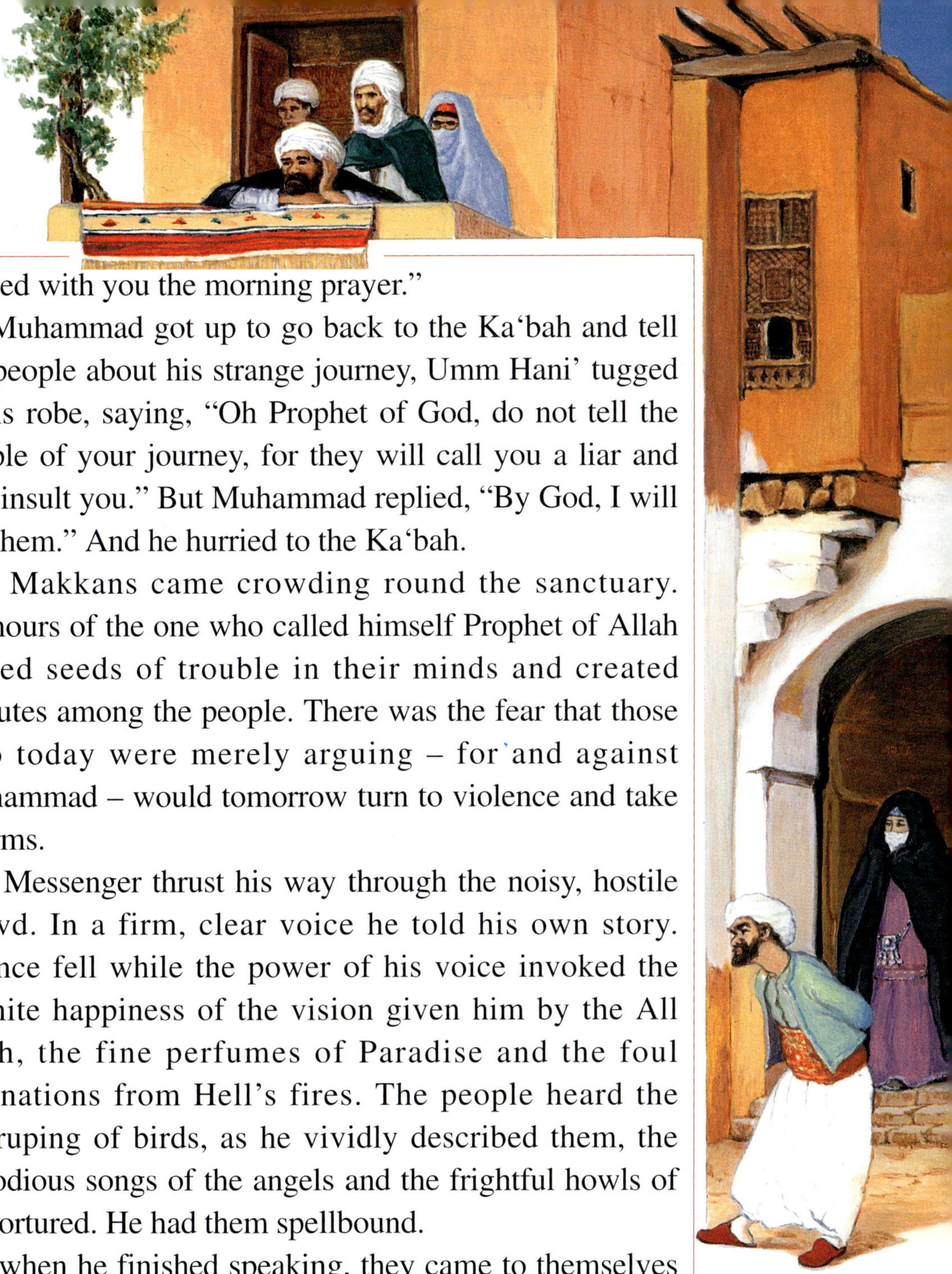

As Muhammad got up to go back to the Ka'bah and tell the people about his strange journey, Umm Hani' tugged at his robe, saying, "Oh Prophet of God, do not tell the people of your journey, for they will call you a liar and will insult you." But Muhammad replied, "By God, I will tell them." And he hurried to the Ka'bah.

The Makkans came crowding round the sanctuary. Rumours of the one who called himself Prophet of Allah sowed seeds of trouble in their minds and created disputes among the people. There was the fear that those who today were merely arguing – for and against Muhammad – would tomorrow turn to violence and take to arms.

The Messenger thrust his way through the noisy, hostile crowd. In a firm, clear voice he told his own story. Silence fell while the power of his voice invoked the infinite happiness of the vision given him by the All High, the fine perfumes of Paradise and the foul emanations from Hell's fires. The people heard the chirruping of birds, as he vividly described them, the melodious songs of the angels and the frightful howls of the tortured. He had them spellbound.

But when he finished speaking, they came to themselves

A small group of Makkans believed implicitly in Muhammad's message, but many, especially among the most powerful, sensed a threat to the established order. It was only in the year 630 that the people of Quraysh recognised the Prophet's authority.

Many were those who that day rallied to Islam.

again. How could such mysteries, so far beyond understanding, so far from things known on earth, ever be believed? But Abu Bakr believed that what his lifelong friend spoke of with such burning faith was true. He exhorted his companions to relax the vice-like grip of doubt that prevented them from understanding things of the spirit.

Faithful friend of Muhammad, Abu Bakr was known as Al-Siddiq, which in Arabic means very sincere.

"So be it," the men of Quraysh agreed, "but let Muhammad describe Jerusalem to us since he says he was there."

They thought this would be the end of this false prophet's ridiculous claim. Muhammad paused. He had seen very little of Jerusalem, only the wall around the Temple and the sanctuary, and all at the dead of night.

Then God rescued his servant. He ordered Gabriel to go and fetch Jerusalem, with its mountains and valleys and streets. In the hand of the angel the entire city took up no more space than a child's toy. Gabriel held it for Muhammad to see, but visible to him alone, so that he was able to depict it in convincing detail. But the Makkans would not admit defeat.

"If you truly covered in one night's journey a distance that has never taken less than thirty days, you will not

have failed to see one of our caravans returning. Can you tell us what goods it brings and if we can hope to see it soon in Makkah?"

The Prophet knew nothing of the caravan but he knew God's power was infinite. He put his trust in Him and bowed his head in prayer. When he looked up he answered: "Your caravan consisted of forty camels, ten for bread, ten for dates, ten for dried figs and ten for raisins. They will arrive here this very day."

Not long after he spoke these words the Makkans heard children shouting and saw a cloud of dust on the horizon that confirmed what Muhammad had said. The caravan was indeed approaching the walls of the town. Faced with such a marvel, few persisted in their hostility.

The Muslims stood respectfully around their guide and praised God. They made sure that the Prophet's account was recorded and later set down in writing in witness of his strange adventure and so that future generations, and all mankind, might know the story of Muhammad's Night Journey.

Abu Bakr, regarded as the first adult male convert, was the first caliph to succeed Muhammad. He is the standing figure, in this 11th-century Persian miniature.

Below, the Angel Gabriel and Muhammad on Mount Hira (here depicted in a Persian miniature). The words which the Angel brought became the Qur'an, meaning recitation.

Islam distinguishes between two kinds of prophet: a rasul, or messenger, who experiences a major revelation, and a nabi, or prophet, whose mission is part of an existing religion. Adam, Noah, Abraham, Ishmael, Moses, Jesus and Muhammad are among the messengers.

Right, a caravan resting.

What do we know of Muhammad?

Left, Bahira met the young Muhammad in Syria. Bahira told Muhammad that he would be God's Messenger.

Tomb of the Prophet, Madinah.

The Muslim calendar begins in 622. The Muslim year 1417 began in July 1996.

Muhammad was born in Makkah in about 570, into the important Quraysh tribe, whose fortunes were made in the caravan trade. His family was not one of the more wealthy branches of the tribe, but they were in charge of the well of Zamzam, supplying water to pilgrims. Muhammad's early life became more difficult after his parents died. He was entrusted to an uncle, Abu Talib, who helped him. Muhammad was a herdsman, then a caravaneer in the service of a rich widow, Khadija, whom he later married.

The revelation

When Muhammad was about forty, he went to Mount Hira to meditate, and the Angel Gabriel first appeared to him, revealing the Word of God. Muhammad memorised the words, to recite them faithfully later.

Only a few Makkans welcomed his news; it brought about a radical break with what the revelation called the jahiliyya, the time of paganism and ignorance; it upset the established order. Relations became worse to the point when, in 622, the Prophet and his companions had to leave the town for the oasis of Yathrib, later known as Madinah, 350 km north of Makkah. That date marks the beginning of the Muslim era. It is the Hijrah, literally 'the emigration'.

Muhammad led the community; and his authority and prestige grew. After battles, which the Prophet's forces won, relations with Makkah improved. Muhammad died in Madinah in 632.

33

Qur'anic tradition and popular Islam

A Muslim (the word means believer) lives with the Qur'an every moment of his life. Below: a Qur'anic school.

The Muslim religion is based on two sources: the Qur'an and the Sunnah.

The Qur'an, holy book of Muslims
For Muslims the Qur'an is the Word of God, transmitted by the Archangel Gabriel to Muhammad. It has 114 chapters, or surats. The Qur'an was memorised in the Prophet's lifetime. Later, in the reign of Caliph Uthman (644-656), a final written version was established; this has remained unchanged.

The Sunnah and the Hadiths
The Qur'an offers much guidance about how the community of believers should be run, but not every detail is given. To supply detail the elders turned to the example of the Prophet, his life and conduct – the Sunnah – and to his judgments and declarations. The Hadiths are reports through which the Sunnah is known.

The Journey: from the Qur'an to the Tradition
The Night Journey, one of the best known episodes in the Prophet's life,

The Qur'an was revealed, written and transmitted in Arabic, so the original Arabic version is sacred. Translations are thus considered a translation of the meaning of the Divine Word, and not a substitute for it.

In Muslim countries teaching is based on the Qur'an and the Tradition. The best students in the Qur'anic schools learn the Qur'an by heart.

To depict living beings, and particularly the Prophet's face, is forbidden in Islam. Some traditions have often broken the rule – for instance in the many Persian miniatures illustrating the Night Journey and other episodes of the Prophet's life.

From the 8th century Islam enjoyed a golden age for 500 years producing erudite scholars and great thinkers. (Left: group of doctors, Persian miniature)

he taste for the marvellous, and for stories heard or told, is an essential feature of the Arab world, to which we owe *The Thousand and One Nights*.

Top of page, a group in conversation, from a Persian miniature of the 13th century.

Tradition has it that this mysterious episode in the life of the Prophet took place on the 7th of the month of Rajab in the year 620.

a sage begging, from a Mogul miniature of the 16th century.

is referred to in a few short verses in the Qur'an. Specialists agree that the 'place of the sanctuary' cited in the Qur'an is Jerusalem. This interpretation – of a journey to what was to become the third holy city of Islam – became accepted.
Detailed accounts of the Journey are found in books of The Hadith – sayings and deeds of Muhammad. Storytellers later used these accounts in their stories, adding their own tales and marvels drawn from earlier traditions or foreign sources. The story tells how Muhammad was spirited away to Jerusalem (isra') and goes on to the climbing of the ladder (mi'raj), the meeting with Allah and the visit to Paradise and to Hell.

A success from the start
The first accounts of the Journey began to circulate from the 7th century. Beyond the attraction of its wonders, the accounts served a political purpose: for believers, a genuine claim of the truth of Islam. In a period of expansion and religious conquest the Journey upholds Muhammad's legitimacy, showing that he was admitted into the presence of God. It confirms his primacy over the prophets of other revealed religions.
The embellished stories told by the story-tellers were passed on down the generations in their romantic form, to the displeasure of those Muslims who promoted a strict reading of the Qur'anic texts and who disliked the images inspired by the tales.

A bridge between East and West
The Journey spread ripples beyond Islam. In the 13th century a Castillian and Latin version appeared entitled *Book of the Ladder of Muhammad*: this was translated into Old French. Its success led to a knowledge of the East by the West. The Italian poet Dante (1265–1321) took inspiration from it for his Divine Comedy, to describe Paradise and the circles of Hell.

"To each his way, on which he fares alone. Every being is unique, and unique also is his relationship with God." Ibn Arabi, a mystic of the 13th century.

Scribes are the guardians of the Tradition.

Mystics see in the Journey an evocation in images of the pilgrimage of the human soul in its search for God.

Left: the Night Journey of Muhammad, from a miniature of the 16th century.

The religions of the Book

In 623 Muhammad and the Muslims, instead of turning towards Jerusalem to pray, turned towards the Ka'bah, the first house built on earth for the worship of Allah.

In mosques this direction is indicated by a niche in the wall, the mihrab.

The Peoples of the Book means Jews, Christians and Muslims, whose faith is based on a single Book – the Bible. For Muslims, its teaching is confirmed and completed in the Koran: "We have revealed to you the Book and the Truth to confirm the Scriptures that came before it." Qur'an, 5, 48.

Many beliefs co-existed in Arabia early in the 7th century. Some people worshipped raised stones, others worshipped creation gods, and some believed in spirits said to dwell in springs or high places.

However, the idea of one God was not unknown. Jewish and Christian communities living in the peninsula were monotheistic – believing in a single god.

One message for three religions

While denouncing polytheist cults, Isalm was more tolerant towards the Peoples of the Book, Jews and Christians who were thought to have already received part of the revelation that the Qur'an was to complete.

But gradually, as the new religion became more defined, it separated from Judaism and Christianity. Differences were revealed and mutual misunderstanding grew. The Qur'an accused Jews and Christians of having changed the nature of the divine message brought to them. Eventually there was war with the Jews of Madinah, who were driven out or killed.

The condition of dhimmis

The following centuries saw a great expansion of Islam. A statute was specified for Jewish and Christian people living under Muslim authority, namely dhimmis. Such people could practise their own religion but had to pay special taxes and, in some areas, wear distinctive garments.

Left, top of page, the profession of faith that admits a person to the Muslim community: "There is no God but Allah and Muhammad is the messenger of Allah."

A Muslim is forbidden to abandon his religion, but conversions to Islam are welcomed.

At various times and in different places some Muslim sovereigns let Jews and Christians hold high office; others restricted them in certain circumstances.

Muhammad foretold that Jesus will come at the end of time to correct wrong additions to his teaching, and to bring about universal peace. (Left, the return of Jesus, after a 16th-century Turkish manuscript.)

Top of page, the sanctuary of Makkah.

The Black Stone, symbol of eternity, is set in a mount of silver. Its colour is said to reflect the sins of mankind.

Makkah was in the 7th century already a busy place of pilgrimage because of the Ka'bah, in and around which numerous idols were kept.

The whole perimeter of Makkah is sacred: only Muslims may enter. Nowadays, as many as 2 million people each year make the pilgrimage to Makkah from all over the world.

Makkah and Madinah

Islam's three sacred cities are Makkah, Madinah and Jerusalem. Makkah is in an enclosed, arid valley. The inhabitants, finding the land poor, exploited the town's position where trade routes crossed. They made fortunes from caravans carrying gold, ivory and slaves from Africa, spices and textiles from the East, perfumes from Arabia, and weapons and cereals from all around the Mediterranean.

A stone from the sky

The holiness of the place goes back to the beginnings of the human race. Adam built the temple of the Ka'bah to house a large white stone that fell from the sky bearing a promise of salvation – consolation for exile from Paradise. Saved from the Flood by the Angel Gabriel, the stone was replaced in the Ka'bah by Abraham and his son Ishmael when they rebuilt the sanctuary. The stone is said to have been blackened by people's sins.

The Ka'bah (meaning cube) is the centre of the Great Mosque of Makkah, the place of pilgrimage (hajj) above all others, that each Muslim should visit at least once. Muhammad led the first pilgrimage in 629.

An ancient place of pilgrimage

Pilgrimage to Makkah involves a series of rites that are performed in and around the Great Mosque over several days. It takes place from the 8th to the 13th of the month of Dhu al-hijjah at the end of the Muslim year. Near the Ka'bah, pilgrims gather by the source of the Zamzam river which God, according to the Bible and Islamic tradition, made well up in the desert to save Ishmael's life, when Abraham had driven him and his mother away.

The original name of Madinah was Yathrib. It was in this oasis, famed for its date palms, that the Prophet found refuge after the Hijrah, earning it the name of Madinat an-Nabi, town of the Prophet. Muhammad established the first Muslim state there.

The Prophet's tomb and the tombs of the first three caliphs are at Madinah. The first mosque, the masjid al-Taqwa, was built here (above, from a Turkish miniature).

Left, pilgrims at Makkah wear a white garment for sanctity.

Top of page –
1: Mosque Al-Aqsa
2: Dome of the Rock
3: West Wall

Today 393,000 Jews, 151,000 Muslims and 15,000 Christians live in Jerusalem east and west.

Jerusalem: holy city of three religions

King David brought the Ark of the Covenant to Jerusalem, spiritual capital of Judaism.

Centre: Dome of the Rock.

The Wall, only relic of the old Temple, is sacred to Judaism.

Triumphant entry of Christ into Jerusalem, from an Arab painting.

Jerusalem is at the heart of the Israel-Arab conflict. Jews and Palestinians claim the same territory. The city was split from 1949 to 1967. It is now under Israeli control.

The Rock (19th century painting)

The three monotheist religions – Judaism, Christianity and Islam – see Jerusalem as the centre of the world. For some, it is the point from which the created world emerged and the place of the Last Judgment. In the Bible, it was on Mount Moriah that God asked Abraham to sacrifice his son Isaac. Abraham's elder son, Ishmael, born of a union with the servant Agar, became father of the Muslims.

The city of David and the Temple

Each religion developed its own tradition. For Jews, Jerusalem is Yerushalahim, the city of peace. About 1000 BC King David chose it as his capital, symbolic of the unity of the twelve tribes of Israel, and he had the holy Ark of the Covenant brought there. Solomon built the temple that was destroyed in 587 BC when Nebuchadnezzar took the town; it was rebuilt and then in AD 70 destroyed by the Romans.

City where Christ died

For Christians, Jerusalem frames the life of Jesus: the nativity story is set in Bethlehem not far away and Jerusalem was the scene of Christ's torture and death.

Point of departure for Heaven

The Night Journey of Muhammad has made Jerusalem especially holy for Islam. It is commemorated by the Dome of the Rock and the mosque Al-Aqsa (meaning: the furthest away), both built at the end of the 7th century. The former was where al-Buraq took off on her flight, and the Rock is said to retain the imprint of her hoof. Jerusalem was the direction in which Muslims turned in prayer until 623 when the direction was changed to the holy city of Makkah.

Top of page: Muhammad's troops confront Byzantine troops (from a Persian miniature). Jihad means the inner ritual battle to control oneself or to resist evil and to defend what is right. It takes the form of physical fighting only when necessary.

Not all Muslims are Arabs, and not all Arabs are Muslims as is seen, for example, in the case of Christian communities of the Lebanon (Maronite and Greek Orthodox) and the Egyptian Copts.

Above, prayer time in a Marseilles street and, right, an Indonesian school.

Islam today

An expanding religion

After the Prophet's death Muslims were set on expansion. The entire Arab peninsular was now under the Islamic state and Muslims spread along the shores of the Mediterranean through Palestine and Egypt, then to provinces of the Byzantine Empire. Later they reached Central Asia. In the 8th century the Mahgreb (Algeria, Tunisia, Morocco) was overcome. In the 12th and 13th centuries Arab merchants took Islam to India, Indonesia and black Africa.

During the same period, the Mongols converted to Islam, building a vast empire from the China Sea to the Baltic. In the 18th century the Ottoman Turks and Persians, also Muslims, shared out the Middle East.

One person in five is a Muslim

Of the 5,000 million human beings alive today, 1,000 million are Muslims. Of the most densely populated countries six are Muslim: Indonesia, Pakistan, Bangladesh, Turkey, Iran, Egypt.

A return to traditional values

Two tendencies challenge one another in all Muslim countries: a fascination with Western values (advances in technology, consumer goods) on the one hand, and fidelity to traditional Islamic values on the other. Traditionalists believe that the problems in Muslim societies today are due to forgetting the Prophet's teachings. But for some the return to the original sources can mix with modern living, while others look back to the exemplary standards of the community of 7th-century Madinah.

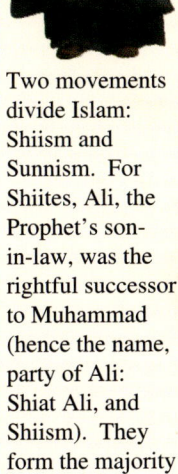

Two movements divide Islam: Shiism and Sunnism. For Shiites, Ali, the Prophet's son-in-law, was the rightful successor to Muhammad (hence the name, party of Ali: Shiat Ali, and Shiism). They form the majority in Iran but represent only 10% of all Muslims.

Look out for other titles in this series:

SARAH, WHO LOVED LAUGHING
A TALE FROM THE BIBLE

THE SECRETS OF KAIDARA
AN ANIMIST TALE FROM AFRICA

I WANT TO TALK TO GOD
A TALE FROM ISLAM

THE RIVER GODDESS
A TALE FROM HINDUISM

CHILDREN OF THE MOON
YANOMAMI LEGENDS

I'LL TELL YOU A STORY
TALES FROM JUDAISM

THE PRINCE WHO BECAME A BEGGAR
A BUDDHIST TALE

JESUS SAT DOWN AND SAID...
THE PARABLES OF JESUS

SAINT FRANCIS, THE MAN WHO SPOKE TO BIRDS
TALES OF ST FRANCIS OF ASSISI

THE MAGIC OF CHRISTMAS
CHRISTMAS TALES FROM EUROPE